Connell Short Guide
to
Cormac McCarthy's

———————

The Road

———————

by
David Isaacs

Contents

NOTES

Introduction

The Road is about a man and a boy trudging through a wasteland after the fall of civilisation.

Shortly after its publication in 2006, the American cultural critic Steven Shaviro wrote, "the novel actively repels commentary; it is so utterly self-contained, so hermetically sealed unto itself, that anything anybody does say about it is both superfluous and wrong". In a review for the *New Republic* the influential literary critic James Wood had a similar warning against trying to find meaning in the book: "*The Road* is not a science fiction, not an allegory, and not a critique of the way we live now." And yet no single novel published in the last ten years has inspired the volume of critical writing that McCarthy's short book has, nor has been studied as much around the world. Shaviro and Wood – and they are not the only ones – are right to be cautious. But it seems the novel actively attracts commentary and does say something about the way we live now.

So how to write about the man and the boy without being superfluous and wrong? One of Cormac McCarthy's great influences is the early 20th century novelist and short story writer Ernest Hemingway. When asked to explain the meaning of his story *The Old Man and the Sea* – in which an old man, urged on by a young boy, goes to sea and catches a gigantic fish, only for it to be eaten by

1

sharks – he had this to say:

> "No good book has ever been written that has in it symbols arrived at beforehand and stuck in... I tried to make a real old man, a real boy, a real sea and a real fish and real sharks. But if I made them good and true enough they would mean many things."

The Road is a mysterious novel; it asks many more questions than it answers. Rather than looking for answers – for meaning – it's probably more fruitful to ask questions about the man, boy and wasteland – about their world – and to see if McCarthy has made them good and true enough that they mean many things.

A summary of the plot

Not much happens in *The Road*. It is set in a future America, around ten years after some apocalyptic event has wiped out all animals, vegetation, and the entirety of civilisation. The dire conditions of life have forced the majority of those few people left alive into savagery and cannibalism. They gang together, hunt, kill and eat anyone who crosses their paths.

A man and his son are walking along America's roads, heading to the coast, looking for a warmer climate and trying to hide from anyone who might do them harm. They carry what few possessions they have in an old shopping trolley and survive by eating tinned food they scavenge from ruined towns. The boy's mother killed herself not long after the unnamed catastrophic event, leaving the man and boy with only two bullets left in their gun: one for each of them. They are – the man tells his son – "the good guys." The rest are "bad guys".

On their journey they encounter many dangers, but also make some welcome discoveries: an underground bunker full of food and drink, for instance. When they reach the sea, the situation does not improve, so they head back inland. The man, who has been showing signs of illness, dies and the boy is approached by a family who seem, remarkably, to be other "good guys". The novel ends as the boy walks off with them, to an uncertain future.

What have they lost?

We never find out how the world ends. McCarthy gives us little to go on: "The clocks stopped at 1:17. A long shear of light and then a series of low concussions"(54)*. That's all we get. In interview

* Page numbers in the text are taken from the edition of the novel published by Alfred A. Knopf (New York) in 2006.

he is dismissive of any attempt to get to the bottom of it, as in this answer he gave to the *Wall Street Journal*:

> A lot of people ask me. I don't have an opinion. [Some scientist friends] said it looked like a meteor to them. But it could be anything – volcanic activity, or it could be nuclear war. It is not really important. The whole thing now is, what do you do?

Plenty of commentators have seen *The Road* as a cautionary tale about climate change. In *The Guardian*, George Monbiot described it as "the most important environmental book ever written"; the critic Chris Danta called it "a profound ecological fable". They may be right. To deny *The Road*'s relevance to discussions about the climate and man's relationship with the environment would be short-sighted. But there is nothing in the novel to suggest the catastrophic event was man-made* or avoidable; it neither blames us nor suggests there's anything we could have done to stop it. And, as McCarthy's answer suggests, it is not really the point, anyway.

---

* The critic Carl James Grindley suggests there's textual evidence that it is not man-made but God-made: it is eerily close, he says, to the apocalypse as described in the Bible. Both "include fire from heaven, the trees and the grass all burned up, ships destroyed, all sea life dead, the sun and the moon blotted out, and so on".

So what is the point? Novels don't exist in vacuums,* and once the question of how and why the world ended recedes, a clearer picture emerges of what real-world events *The Road* might be a response to. James Wood has suggested it's a "9/11 novel that is pretending not to be a 9/11 novel". Many critics agree. In his book *The American Nightmare*, the Turkish critic Özden Sözalan argues that the terrorist attacks on the World Trade Centre mark the point at which the American Dream became the American Nightmare; American novelists have accordingly shifted their focus from dream to nightmare. He fashions his argument around two novels: *The Road* and Don Delillo's *Falling Man*. For Delillo, 9/11 was a kind of "end of America" and his novel asks the question: "What comes after America?" "There's an empty space," one of his characters says, "where America used to be."

The man and the boy in *The Road* occupy that space. American ruins litter their landscape. They pass "billboards advertising motels" (6); "coins everywhere in the ash" (22); "small pleasureboats half sunken in the gray water" (24); "a burned house, just the brick chimney standing in in the

---

* Cormac McCarthy's novels in particular are often written in response to world events. His masterpiece, *Blood Meridian* – which follows, in gory detail, a band of cowboys massacring innocent people around the United States/Mexico border in the mid-18th century – was written in the wake of Vietnam, and deals with the national mood in America during and after that war.

yard" (107); "a once grand house sited on a rise above a road" (111). McCarthy has always written about founding American myths; here, post 9/11, he has created a myth of its destruction.

Often the man tries to recreate this old world for the boy, but to the boy it means nothing. They come across an abandoned train, for example, and the man climbs into the driver's seat. "He made train noises and diesel horn noises but he wasn't sure what these might mean to the boy"(192). Or, walking through a ruined house, he finds a phone, picks it up, pretends to dial a number. "The boy watched him. What are you doing? he said"(5). At one point, the man comes across an upturned "softdrink machine" (22) in which he finds an unopened can of coke. The boy has no idea what it is; it seems miraculous.

Recognisable and banal to us, to the boy these are mysterious relics from another world, like the ruins of Greece or Egypt in ours. For the boy, the real – our real – has become mythic. He regards these remains with a fascination that is alien to us. As the novelist Jennifer Egan pointed out in *Slate*, the boy "talks of crows, the sun... and the blue sea with the same mythical longing one hears in today's children's talk of queens and dragons". The novel destabilises the apparent solidity of our world; what we take for granted, the novel says, is transient and mortal. A can of coke as relic and miracle: it is hard to read *The Road* and not see the world with new eyes.

The most prominent American ruin in the novel is, of course, the road itself, which critics often read as a metonym* for capitalism. The road, its original purpose, its history and its connotations are all mysteries to the boy, who has probably never heard of capitalism or Henry Ford. Showing the boy his map – itself a symbol of existing within a community – the man tries to explain it:

> *These are our roads, the black lines on the map.*
> *The state roads.*
> *Why are they state roads?*
> *Because they used to belong to the states. What used to be called the states.*
> *But there's not any more states? No.*
> *What happened to them?*
> *I don't know exactly. That's a good question.*
> *But the roads are still there.*
> *Yes. For a while.*
> *How long a while?*
> *I don't know. (43)*

All these relics and ruins speak not only of a dead civilisation but also of a dead – or dying – language; one of McCarthy's ongoing

---

* A metonym is a kind of metaphor in which a part of something is used to refer to its whole – for example, "Hollywood" meaning the American film industry, or "the suits" referring to the club managers at a football match.

preoccupations. (A brief diversion into 19th century Swiss linguistics: the 19th century Swiss linguist Ferdinand de Saussure posited an enormously influential theory of language. As Saussure conceived it, language is made up of signs: words are signs, but other things can be signs, too. The can of coke, the billboards, the pleasure boats, the road – they're all signs, of a kind. They represent things beyond themselves. For Saussure a sign has two sides to it, like a coin: the *signifier* and the *signified*. The signifier is the word (or image) itself: its shape, its sound, its appearance. The signified is what it represents – the image or concept that appears in our mind when we hear or see the signifier.)

The world of *The Road* is one full of empty signs: that is, signifiers (words, objects etc...) that have nothing left to signify; signifier cut adrift from signified. Words remain, but the things they represent don't; there are more words than things. At one point the man and boy come across an "advertisement in faded ten-foot letters across [a] roofslope. See Rock City"(20). Rock City is long gone, and in the way it explicitly draws its reader's attention to something no longer there, this advertisement functions as a metonym for language in a post-apocalyptic world. Language and meaning are disconnected. In McCarthy's words, "Everything uncoupled from its shoring"(10).

One response to a world with a superfluity of

language is a desire for silence. And, indeed, when the man remembers the perfect day from his childhood, a day spent collecting firewood with his uncle, it is significant that what he hones in on is how neither of them "had spoken a word... This is the day to shape the days upon"(12). As such, over the course of the novel the man and the boy say very little to one another. And when they do speak, it is usually for a purpose: to ask a question, to answer a question, to give a command, to express trepidation.

In one of the most famous passages from the book, the man tries to speak but finds he has nothing to say:

> *He tried to think of something to say but he could not. He'd had this feeling before, beyond the numbness and the dull despair. The world shrinking down about a raw core of parsible entities. The names of things slowly following those things into oblivion. Colors. The names of birds. Things to eat. Finally the names of things one believed to be true. More fragile than he would have thought. How much was gone already? The sacred idiom shorn of its referents and so of its reality. Drawing down like something trying to preserve heat. In time to wink out forever. (93)*

This difficult passage describes the process by which words, cut adrift from the real objects, people, places, thoughts, feelings that they once described, are beginning to disappear themselves. It's a tricky concept to grasp, so here's a thought experiment. Think of the word "green". Think of the colour that word refers to. Now imagine trying to explain that colour to a blind person, without actually using the word "green". You probably can't. Now imagine a world from which the colour green has been removed. There are still people alive who remember what the colour green was. But they can't explain it to their children. And one day, when no-one who remembers the colour green is left, the word "green" will just be an unanchored sound bobbing around, meaning nothing. After that, it will be gone.

What's the connection between a lost language and a lost state? The mid-20th century French philosopher Michel Foucault may have the answer. McCarthy seems to be interested in Foucault's notion of language as a kind of power. For Foucault, language creates and structures thought. Countries, states, create or seize control of their national language. As a result, they have power over national discourse. Language and discourse,* Foucault believed, create and structure truth within a community. To put it succinctly: states create language and language creates truth. In *The Road*,

* That is, an accepted body of thoughts and ideas expressed through language within a specific community (in this case, America).

the state has vanished and language is on its way out.

Where does that leave truth? Has truth vanished, too? Is truth something relative, chained to the people who believe it, something that differs depending on who or where you are? Or is truth something transcendent and objective; a fixed, unchanging reality? Is reality, in other words, created by language? McCarthy's novels are peopled with characters who believe both – from a church caretaker in *The Crossing,* who says "this world which seems to us a thing of stone and flower and blood is not a thing at all but is a tale", to the cowboy John Grady Cole in *All the Pretty Horses* who, in response to the suggestion from his girlfriend that "everything is talk" replies: "Not everything." McCarthy himself has not offered an answer.

Before moving on to discuss what the man and the boy have, it is important to stress that the world has not ended. All is not lost. As Margaret Atwood recently said, in relation to her trilogy of post-apocalyptic novels, *MaddAddam*, you "can't actually wipe out the human race and then tell a story about it. There has to be somebody still alive through whom you can hear that story. It's like that conundrum of where will I go after I die. You're still imagining an 'I'." There is no such thing as *post-apocalypse*.

And, strictly speaking, McCarthy is not writing about endings. He's writing – and always has been – about entropy. There's a difference. Entropy – a

11

term used in physics – is the movement from order to disorder. It is a process, not an ending. It's not a good process, and McCarthy doesn't seem to think there's much hope of reversal. In fact, he regards the idea that things might get better as a dangerous, fettering one. He famously said in an interview with the *New York Times* in 1992:

> There's no such thing as life without bloodshed...
> I think the notion that the species can be improved in some way, that everyone could live in harmony, is a really dangerous idea. Those who are afflicted with this notion are the first ones to give up their souls and their freedom. Your desire that it be that way will enslave you and make your life vacuous.

The Road is just another stage in what McCarthy sees as the inevitable worsening of the world. McCarthy's interest has always been in a particular kind of entropy: cultural entropy. For McCarthy, with the gradual rise of capitalism and the homogenisation of culture, the world has lost something – a sense of community, of tradition, of human interconnectedness. As such, his novels always look back to a lost happiness. Philip Connors wrote in the *London Review of Books*: "In McCarthy there is almost always a time before and a time after, a lost world and a baffling or disappointed new one." *The Road* is the only novel

of his in which this is made literal.

In his introduction to David Holloway's book *The Late Modernism of Cormac McCarthy*, Rick Wallach wrote: "The narratives anticipate the exhaustion and failure of culture at every turn... he shows us these things in the process of being laid waste." Holloway's book was published four years before *The Road*, but it seems prescient. Wallach describes what McCarthy is reacting against as "the sludgy sameness – literary, musical, cinematic, economic and political – of the ethos of late capitalism". "Sludgy sameness" – doesn't that sound exactly like the physical landscape of *The Road*? Could it be that *The Road* is a metaphor for the sameness of modern culture?

What do they have?

So the world of *The Road* has lost America. Language and meaning have also been partially severed, "uncoupled", both from each other and from the control of a state which no longer exists, and both are therefore left free-floating. But we have not lost language nor meaning; they are shrinking and morphing, "drawing down like something trying to preserve heat", but they still exist. One day they will "wink out forever"; but when that will happen is not something *The Road* addresses.

These philosophical concerns are a significant part of the book's weft, but at its heart it is a novel about a father and son; about their experience of life together; about their day-to-day existence. Remember McCarthy's comments about the nature of the catastrophic event: "It is not really important. *The whole thing now is, what do you do?*" Answer: you survive. *The Road* is a novel about how you survive.

The man and boy have survived as long as they have because of the man's almost supernatural pragmatism. There are suggestions in the novel that he may have been a doctor in a past life.[*]

[*] When explaining to a man he's about to shoot that the man won't be able to hear the bullet, he says "the bullet travels faster than sound. It will be in your brain before you can hear it. To hear it you will need a frontal lobe and things with names like colliculus and temporal gyrus and you wont have them anymore. They'll just be soup"(67). Impressed by his knowledge of the human brain, the man asks: "Are you a doctor?" "I'm not anything," he responds.

Whether he was or not, he certainly knows what the human body needs to survive. Just moments after the "long shear of light", he is using his immediate environment to fight for survival: "He went into the bathroom and threw the lightswitch but the power was already gone... He dropped to one knee and raised the lever to stop the tub and then turned on both taps as far as they would go"(54). When his wife enters the room, she asks why he's running a bath. "I'm not," he says. He is making sure they have a supply to hand. Survival is an instinct. The boy is lucky to have him.

In *The Road*, existence is stripped to its bare essentials. As Grace Hellyer has it, "all objects have more or less shifted into the two categories of the useful and the redundant". The difference between life and death is pragmatism; pragmatism is all there is. Thus the vast majority of the novel is given over to detailing, minutely and coolly, the physical tasks the man undertakes to survive. This is a typical passage:

In the service bay he dragged out the steel trashdrum and tipped it over and pawed out all the quart plastic oilbottles. Then they sat in the floor decanting them of their dregs one by one, leaving the bottles to stand upside down draining into a pan until at the end they had almost a half quart of motor oil. He screwed down the plastic cap and wiped the bottle off with a rag and hefted it in his hand. Oil for their little

slutlamp to light the long gray dusks, the long gray
dawns. You can read me a story, the boy said. Can't
you, Papa? Yes, he said. I can. (6)

Important to note that the boy's request for a story
reads like a continuation of the list-like account of
decanting oil, as if storytelling and pragmatism are
one and the same. We'll come back to that.
Elsewhere, routine activity – pushing the cart,
making fires, looking through binoculars – is
described in the same language as moments of
sheer horror. The man accepts both with equal
stoicism – as when he shoots a man who has taken
hold of his son threateningly and afterwards has to
wash the boy: "This is my child, he said. I wash a
dead man's brains out of his hair. That is my
job"(77). The routine, the horrific, and the make-
believe share the same space in *The Road*. All is
survival, all is pragmatism.

Or not quite all: they have each other. Father
and son – "shuffling through the ash, each the
other's world entire" (4) – have a bond that
transcends pure pragmatism. From the novel's first
words, this bond is made powerfully present:
"When he woke in the woods in the dark and the
cold of the night he'd reach out to touch the child
sleeping beside him"(1). His first instinct, on
waking, is not his own survival: it is to check that
his son is still alive.

The Road is at its most poignant when

describing the man's attempts to give his son a proper upbringing in the midst of an apocalyptic wasteland. Trying to teach him to swim, for example: "He held him and floated him about, the boy gasping and chopping at the water. You're doing good, the man said. You're doing good" (39). Or cutting his hair: "He sat the boy on the footlocker under the gaslamp and with a plastic comb and a pair of scissors he set about cutting his hair. He tried to do a good job and it took some time... He cut his own hair but it didn't come out so good"(161). Significantly, the care with which he cuts his son's hair is lacking when he cuts his own. The most heart-breaking image in the novel comes when they reach the sea, and the man lets the boy run into it:

He stood naked, clutching himself and dancing. Then he went running down the beach. So white. Knobby spinebones. The razarous shoulder blades sawing under the pale skin. Running naked and leaping and screaming into the slow roll of the surf. (233)

Such an ordinary scene; who can't remember running excitedly into the sea as a child? But in this new, uncanny context the ordinary is made strange. Our childhoods suddenly seem a bit more special. This is a world in which the facts of life – the things we take for granted – are intensified, "so that routine occurrences", as the influential American critic Harold Bloom has said, "take on an almost existential importance".

Beyond being emotionally wrenching, these scenes of displaced domesticity are significant in their ritualistic, quasi-religious function. When the man washes a dead man's brains from his son's hair, for example, it is described in explicitly religious terms: "He sat holding him while he tousled his hair before the fire to dry it. All of this like some ancient anointing"* (78). In his guide to *The Road,* Harold Bloom writes:

> The presentation of [the bond between father and son] through the practice of small, routine acts, a practice that could be described as sacramental, is crucial in a world in which such acts and attitudes could easily be overlooked and forgotten; as the narrator observes: "The last instance of a thing takes the class with it." If the father stops acting like a father or the son like a son, then in a sense those bonds and defined roles will be forever lost.

The man is trying to give their existence meaning; there is no point to survival if their lives lack

---

* An anointing is a religious ceremony common to several religions. It usually symbolises the introduction of divine influence. The name "Christ" derives from the Ancient Greek word, Khristòs, which literally means "the anointed one".

meaning. In that sense, it's he who is lucky to have the boy. The boy brings meaning. The novel is littered with examples of the boy giving and helping – examples, in other words, of charity. They come across a man struck by lightning and the boy's immediate response is to ask: "Can we help him Papa?" (51); or, later, they come across the grouchy and gnomic prophet Ely (more of whom later) and the boy insists they share their food with him. The man refuses but the boy argues him round. As Chris Danta has noted, "the boy meets the man's hard, pragmatic individualism with charity and fellow-feeling". The man has the practical know-how to survive; the boy has the goodness and compassion to make that survival worthwhile. This is what they give each other.

One of the questions in the novel – much like the question about the objectivity or subjectivity of truth – is whether goodness and morality are innate or constructed. The man spends much time trying to construct a moral framework for the boy. He tells him "old stories of courage and justice as he remembered them" (42). And it is evident from the number of times the boy asks for reassurance that they're "the good guys" that, as a result of the man's efforts, a rudimentary, binary good guys/bad guys moral code forms part of his consciousness. The 19th-century German philosopher Friedrich Nietzsche thought that the moral laws we live our lives by have no absolute or divine truth or value and that morality is something society has created for pragmatic purposes, in order to ensure its survival. Morality, in other words, is a kind of self-preservation. This, it has been said, is the process we are witnessing in the father and son relationship.

But in an interview with the *Wall Street Journal*, McCarthy suggested that "goodness" cannot be constructed, that it is innate:

> I don't think goodness is something that you learn... If you're left adrift in the world to learn goodness from it, you would be in trouble... There's not much you can do to try to make a child into something he is not. But whatever he is, you can sure destroy it. Just be mean and cruel and you can destroy the best person.

Read against this, it looks like the man is not trying to instil goodness in his son. Rather, he's trying to stop him being corrupted, to stop the boy's innate goodness drowning in the horror that surrounds him. If that were to happen, meaning would drain from their world and there would no longer be any drive to survive. It would be suicide. The religious observation of the father/son rituals and the construction of a moral code do serve a pragmatic purpose, then: they are a kind of self- preservation. In giving them a reason to survive they become a means of survival.

So much for their present. But theirs is not the only present. We, the readers, have our own experience of the novel – we accompany them as they cross the wasteland – and our experience of their experience is just as worthy of exploration.

The Road is full of horror – starvation, disease, kidnap, murder, infanticide, cannibalism – yet on its publication in 2006 it was hailed by critics as a work of extreme beauty. Stephen Fry said it is "a vexing irony" that McCarthy has written "a novel of incomparable beauty derived from the raw matter of incomparable horror". This is generally true of McCarthy's novels, but in most of the others the horror is lightened by the beauty of his writing about nature. The Road adds another dimension: not only is it full of horror, it is also devoid of nature. The critic Chris Danta pointed out in his essay, "'The cold illucid word': The poetics of gray in Cormac McCarthy's *The Road*", that everything is grey:[*]

> *days are gray; dusks are gray; dawns are gray; the light and the sky are gray; the landscape is gray; the city is gray; tree stumps are gray; the ash is gray; the slush, sleet, and ice are gray; the beach, sea, and hagmoss are gray; the water is gray; the window is gray; clothes are gray; the human body, both living and dead, is gray; hair is gray; teeth are gray; viscera*

[*] The word "gray" appears 81 times in the novel – almost once every three pages.

are gray. And last but not least – the heart is gray.

Adam Mars-Jones wrote in his *Observer* review: "Part of the achievement of *The Road* is its poetic description of landscapes from which the possibility of poetry would seem to have been stripped, along with their ability to support life." McCarthy's raw matter is not only incomparable horror, it's also incomparable dullness.

So how does he do it? In his review for the New Republic, James Wood outlined the three registers that make up McCarthy's prose. The first is a kind of "painstaking minimalism". Pages and pages are given over to descriptions of physical actions in minute and unadorned detail. This plain kind of writing – which uses few descriptive words and simple sentence structures – McCarthy owes to Ernest Hemingway. A typical sentence in Hemingway's *The Old Man and the Sea*, reads: "Once he stood up and urinated over the side of the skiff and looked at the stars and checked his course." *The Road* is full of sentences that follow the "he did this and then he did this" pattern (technical word: "parataxis"):

> *He went to the garage and got the knapsack and came back and took a last look around and then went down the steps and pulled the door shut and jammed one of the handles of the pliers through the heavy inside hasp. (150)*

The effect, says the critic John Cant, is to "divert the reader's mind from the anxiety generated through identification with the protagonists in the extremity of their plight, just as it diverts the minds of the characters themselves to be absorbed in practical activity".

The second register, writes James Wood, is an "exquisite, gnarled, slightly antique (and even slightly clunky or heavy) lyricism". These are the moments when the muscular simplicity bubbles into something richer and more descriptive; it is "not only beautiful, but powerfully efficient as poetry". The shape of a city seen from afar, for example, standing "in the grayness like a charcoal drawing sketched across the waste" (7); or his description of ash being blown by the wind: "The soft black talc blew through the streets like squid ink uncoiling along a sea floor" (192-193). This is where most of the novel's aesthetic beauty comes from.

Wood is not such a fan of McCarthy's third register. What some critics praise as his "biblical" language, Wood sees as "merely antiquarian, a kind of vatic histrionic groping in which the prose plumes itself up and flourishes an ostensibly obsolete lexicon". Wood gives as an example a description of the father and son as "slumped and cowled and shivering in their rags like mendicant friars" (133). "Mendicant" is an old word for "begging", and for Wood it's a superfluous and ostentatious anachronism.

Perhaps Wood misses an important effect. It's true that the old-fashioned words scattered through the book are jarring,* but perhaps they are meant to be. As we have seen, *The Road* is in part a book about dead, or dying language. So it is fitting that McCarthy should use obsolete words in his prose. But there is another effect at play: his use of an antique lexicon brings the past into the present, a dead world to life. Conversely, in equating a dead language with our language, it creates the strange feeling that, in *The Road*, all language is ancient. The past is present and the present past: it enacts a flattening, or levelling of time – which is appropriate for a novel about a time after history

As Mark Steven and Julian Murphet observed in their essay, "The charred ruins of a library", the moments of lyrical poetry and antique pronouncement bloom out of the economic minimalism that we associate with Hemingway. The effect, they say, is that, "style appears amid the routine production of narrative sentences like the fossilised prints of an extinct mammal, left in the baking tar eons ago". This third register, in other words, fossilises the world we live in.

---

* And on many occasions they interrupt the reading process while you wait for Google to tell you what the word means. How are we supposed to know that in the sentence "the salitter drying from the earth", salitter is a word used only in the works of the 16th century German mystic Jacob Boehme to mean "God's presence"?

McCarthy's writing is mimetic. "Mimesis" is a process by which prose, poetry and form – their sound, rhythm, placement – enact the thing they are describing. It may not be obvious how that would work, so here are some examples. There are no chapters or paragraphs in *The Road*. The novel is comprised, rather, of short chunks of text – often a few lines long, rarely longer than a page – which are separated from the chunks of text before and after by a gap. The effect is that the book feels like an endless trudge forward, with no clear feeling of progression. It enacts the journey the man and boy undertake: it has no real direction and is little more than a series of repetitive, self-contained moments and incidents.

Equally, the relentless repetition of simple descriptive words ("cold", "dark", "gray") throughout the novel enacts the same flat repetitiousness that the two characters experience in their day-to-day lives. See, for instance, the first few sentences of the novel: "When he woke in the woods in the *dark* and the cold of the night... Nights *dark* beyond *darkness*... Like the onset of some *cold* glaucoma..." (1). In the hands of a lesser writer, the effect would be clunky and numbing; in McCarthy's it is thrilling.

The most significantly mimetic aspect of the novel's prose is the way the structure of the sentences mirrors the destruction of civilisation. Here are two examples: "Lying there in the dark with the uncanny taste of a peach from some phantom orchard fading from his mouth" (17); "a reach of meadowlands stark and gray... Everything as it once had been save faded and weathered"(6). Notice how we read about the "uncanny taste of a peach" before we discover that it's a "phantom". Or we see "a reach of meadowlands" before they become "stark and gray"; "Everything as it once had been" becomes "faded and weathered". The descriptions are split into before and after.

Reading like this, we can't help but call up the image of a green and rolling meadow in our mind's eye, even if only momentarily. Time and time again, McCarthy builds up scenes of American pastoral and burns them down before our very eyes. The technique enacts what the narrator says of the man's dreams: "the dreams so rich in colour... Waking in the cold dawn it all turned to ash instantly. Like certain ancient frescoes entombed for centuries suddenly exposed to the day"(20). Repeatedly we see things vibrant and rich in colour turn to ash instantly. The prose re-enacts the ruination of the world. We *feel* the loss.

To some small degree, then, we are not watching from a distance but sharing the experiences of the man and boy. *Our* experience, however, because of McCarthy's mastery over his style, gives us pleasure. Does that mean we're *enjoying* the misery of others? Perhaps. And it's a troubling question. But most commentators seem to agree that McCarthy's language is in some way redemptive. The writer and critic Robert Macfarlane, in an article in *Intelligent Life,* says that hope "survives in McCarthy's language". Harold Bloom says that "magnificence – [his] language, landscape, persons, conceptions – at last transcends the violence, and converts goriness into terrifying art". And the critic Sean Pryor writes, in his essay "McCarthy's Rhythm", that by imitating the world of *The Road* in the rhythm of the prose, he "redeems the wasteland". This idea is perhaps most neatly expressed by John Cant:

> *The Road* expresses the paradox that lies at the heart of all serious pessimistic literature: its literary passion defies the very emptiness that it proclaims. It declares the inevitability of cultural entropy, but is itself an example of cultural vitality.

McCarthy, however, goes a step further. *The Road* is narrated in the third person, with one or two exceptions. Occasionally he breaks into the first person for a sentence or two, as with the following sequence:

> *The ashes of the late world carried on the bleak and temporal winds to and fro in the void. Carried forth and scattered and carried forth again. Everything uncoupled from its shoring. Unsupported in the ashen air. Sustained by a breath, trembling and*

brief. If only my heart were stone. (10)

Briefly, McCarthy lets the breath of the man –
trembling and brief – enter his prose. Its
effectiveness is its brevity. But at one point he
breaks into the first person for an entire section:

> *The dog that he remembers followed us for two days.
> I tried to coax it to come but it would not. I made a
> noose of wire to catch it. There were three cartridges
> in the pistol. None to spare. She walked away down
> the road. The boy looked after her and then he looked
> at me and then he looked at the dog and he began to
> cry and to beg for the dog's life and I promised I
> would not hurt the dog. A trellis of a dog with the
> hide stretched over it. The next day it was gone. That
> is the dog he remembers. He doesn't remember any
> little boys. (91)*

It is a deeply strange effect. This is not the free
indirect discourse we're so familiar with in the
novel: the novelist weaving the language and
thoughts of a character into a third person
narration. This is pure first person narration. But
who is this ghostly first person addressing? Us?
What have we got to do with anything?

There are other direct addresses to the reader
in the novel: ""Do you think that your fathers are
watching? That they weight you in their
ledgerbook? Against what? There is no book and

your fathers are dead in the ground" (209). Here is another example: "The last instance of a thing takes the class with it. Turns out the light and is gone. Look around you" (29). *Look around you*: can there be a clearer enunciation of what the novel is about? With his prose rhythms, choice of language and sentence structure, McCarthy makes us experience the death of civilisation along with the man and the boy; he draws us into their world and we watch their world burn. And then he jolts us back to the present – to our present – and tells us to look out of the window. It is in the hope, I presume, that we appreciate the view more. Reviewing *The Road* in The Guardian, Alan Warner wrote: "In creating an exquisite nightmare, it does not add to the cruelty and ugliness of our times; it warns us now how much we have to lose."

"Borrowed time and borrowed world and borrowed eyes with which to sorrow it" (138). This is one of the most striking sentences in the novel, and is worth unpicking. *Borrowed time*: human civilisation will not last forever. *Borrowed world*: the world we live in is not ours to do with what we like. *Borrowed eyes with which to sorrow it*: we can only mourn its passing by watching its death through invented eyes – the man's and the boy's. Otherwise it will be too late.

FIVE FACTS ABOUT
Cormac McCarthy and The Road

1. McCarthy changed his first name to Cormac from Charles after a noble ancestor, Cormac Laidir McCarthy, who built Blarney Castle in Ireland.

2. When Oprah Winfrey chose *The Road* for her Book Club in 2008, McCarthy agreed to an interview with her for his first ever television appearance.

3. McCarthy isn't a fan of literary giants. On Henry James and Marcel Proust, he said: "I don't understand them... To me, that's not literature. A lot of writers who are considered good I consider strange."

4. McCarthy used the same Olivetti Lettera 32 typewriter for almost 5o years. On it he wrote nearly all of his novels, screenplays, and correspondence from 1960 to 2009. In 2009 the typewriter was sold for $254,500 at auction.

5. In the 1950s, while stationed with the U.S. Air Force in Alaska, McCarthy hosted a radio show for the troops.

Opposite: A still from John Hillcoat's 2009 film adaptation of The Road.

What do they stand to gain?

If the world is not ours – whose is it? "Perhaps in the world's destruction it would be possible at last to see how it was made," the man hopes (293). No such luck, sadly. He never solves the mystery of creation.

But *The Road* is a novel about America – or post-America – so at least to some extent it must be about Christianity – or *post*-Christianity – too. That's why the book is bursting with Christian imagery. From the first page, the man and boy are presented as if caught in some religious parable: in the opening dream of the cave, they are like "pilgrims in a fable swallowed up and lost among the inward parts of some granitic beast" (1) – a reference to the Bible story of Jonah and the Whale. And from then on the religious references don't let up.

Most of the explicitly Christian images describe the boy, usually from the man's point of view rather than the narrator's. At one point the man describes him in these terms: "Golden chalice, good to house a god."* The most extreme recurring image is of the holy light the boy gives off. Early on: "When he rose and turned to go back the tarp was lit from within where the boy had wakened"(49). Later, he

---

* A reference to the Holy Grail. Significantly, the novel was initially going to be called The Grail (78).

is "glowing in that waste like a tabernacle".* Later still: "when he moved the light moved with him"(296). He is literally giving off light.** What are we to make of this? Is the boy Jesus? Is this some kind of second coming? We surely know McCarthy well enough by now to know that these questions will remain unanswered.

And there is certainly plenty of doubt in the novel. Early on, the man says of the boy: "If he is not the *word* of God God never spoke."*** The way those two conflicting beliefs butt against one another in that sentence ("the word of God"; "God never spoke") and meet at the hard repetition of the word God enacts the dual religious nature of the novel: the co-existence of belief and disbelief; the enduring presence and absence of God.

For that, the most significant episode is the encounter with a man the father and son come across shuffling grumpily through the ash. They ask him his name; he says it's Ely. Ely is short for Elijah, an Old Testament prophet. Later he claims Ely is not his name, but by naming himself as such, however briefly, he is fashioning himself as some kind of prophet. He and the man speak about God; Ely concludes: "There is no God and we are his

* A dwelling-place for divine presence.

** Of course, the man may be going blind, or mad; but, equally, he may not.

*** According to Christian teaching, Jesus is "The Word of God"(3).

33

prophets"(181).* Harold Bloom has called this comment "one of the clearest articulations of the novel's simultaneous disbelief in a divine presence and its fundamental reliance on – or, as could be argued, faith in – religious roles and sacraments in order to create meaning in such a nihilistic universe". Ely is the prophet of God's dual nature.

Even the narrator doesn't seem to know if God exists in this universe. At one stage, the landscape is described as "Barren, silent, godless"(2). Which seems like a fairly firm authorial announcement that there is no God. Later, however, it is "Cold and starless. Blessed"(121). Which sounds like there *is* a God; who else could bless the cold and starless night? But if there is a God in this world, he is certainly not present in his creation; if there is a God, he is a distant, removed God. Often in the novel, the universe is described as if it's conscious:

> *The blackness on those nights was sightless and impenetrable. A blackness to hurt your ears with listening. Often he had to get up.*
>
> *No sound but the wind in the bare and blackened trees. He rose and stood tottering in the cold autistic dark. (14)*

* The Muslim statement of faith – the "Shahada" – is often translated as: "There is no God but Allah, and Mohammed is his prophet." It was playfully twisted in the 1920s when various famous physicists were discussing their views on religion. Paul Dirac, founder of quantum physics, was in the middle of explaining his take (that God is a product of the human imagination), when another physicist, Wolfgang Pauli, interrupted him and said: "There is no God and Dirac is his prophet."

If there is a God, he is "sightless" and "autistic": blind and lacking in empathy.

So nihilism (the belief in an empty and chaotic universe) and Christianity walk side by side in *The Road*, and both pose questions about what a future may look like. At the end of the novel, the boy is rescued by an all-American, Christian family, who take him under their wing and "talk to him sometimes about God"(306). Critics are fiercely divided about whether this represents the boy's salvation (a Christian reading), or a cruel false hope (a nihilistic reading); whether, in other words, this ending suggests hope for the future.

For the man, at least, if not for us, the boy by his very existence represents the promise of some kind of continuation. As the psychoanalyst Adam Phillips and the historian Barbara Taylor pointed out in their book *On Kindness,* children are the future; the child provides the means for "civilising" culture. "When," in Mary Zournazi's phrase, "the world of adults and reason has reached its end... the child acts as the creative potential of the future". In the great South African novelist J.M. Coetzee's novel *The Childhood of Jesus,*[*] the child is described as the "bearer of the future". The importance of this concept to the man in *The Road*

* This novel follows a man and a boy, neither of whom have names, as they try to make sense of a new, apparently post- apocalyptic world. Jesus is never mentioned in the novel, but the boy has a number of similarities to Christ.

is painfully present in his use of the world "always": "We'll always be the good guys."

Regularly, in *The Road*, the man or the boy repeat the phrase, "We're carrying the fire":

> *We're going to be okay, arent we Papa? Yes. We are.*
> *And nothing bad is going to happen to us.*
> *That's right.*
> *Because we're carrying the fire. Yes. Because*
> *we're carrying the fire. (87)*

This mantra suggests a future; it gives their lives direction and their existence purpose. What, exactly, that purpose is – and what the fire represents – is something that has provoked a number of critical discussions, and a number of different interpretations.

But the most likely philosophical precedent for what "the fire" represents is Gnosticism. Gnosticism is a difficult religious philosophy to pin down: it's a term that was first used fairly recently to refer to a diverse pattern of beliefs around the first and second centuries BC. Still, there are some general things to be said about it, and they are central to understanding the works of Cormac McCarthy.

According to Gnostic beliefs – which are generally thought to have arisen as a response to the question of why evil exists in a world created by a benevolent god – the physical world we live in was created not by the Christian God but by an evil force called the demiurge and is ruled over by lesser evil deities called archons. Our world is evil. We're used to philosophers and writers asking: "How can there be evil in a world created by God?" But McCarthy's novels ask, "How can there be good in a world created by evil?" Gnostics answer that question thus: when the demiurge created the material world he trapped sparks of the divine within it. In a gnostic conception of the world, the good and the light are forever trapped inside the evil and the dark. The "hero" is the person who releases these sparks – the soul – and it is by acknowledging their presence that an individual can achieve *gnosis* – or, knowledge of the transcendent realm – that is, the good.

Read against this religious philosophy, the fire that the man and the boy carry within them is a shard of the divine. They are holy grails, golden chalices housing God. They are the heroes. And they are surrounded by evil presences bent on destruction, or *archons*: the villains. In a Gnostic understanding of the universe there is a constant war between good and evil, between light and dark, good guys and bad guys. In *The Road*, darkness is winning. You can see why it may be important that the man and the boy succeed in carrying and passing on the fire: if they have the last remaining sparks of the divine within them, the future of goodness depends on it.

At one point, the boy has a nightmare:

*I had this penguin that you wound up and it would
waddle and flap its flippers. And we were in that
house that we used to live in and it came around the
corner but nobody had wound it up and it was really
scary... The winder wasn't turning. (37)*

The penguin is frightening because it moves
seemingly of its own accord, and yet is purely
automatic, it has nothing in it; no divine spark. It is
a fear of soullessness and mechanisation that the
boy is displaying here. Fear that they are not
carrying the fire.

Later, a group of bad guys marching down the
road are described in similar terms: "They clanked
past, marching with a swaying gait like wind-up
toys"(96). "Were they the bad guys?/Yes they were
the bad guys"(97). The boy is scared, in other
words, that they are not good guys, not carrying the
fire, that there is no fire, there is no God.

Whether or not there is a God, religious
observation is an instinct for the man, just as his
pragmatism is. On many occasions he finds himself
kneeling as to pray, impulsively, often without
realising it:

*Then he just knelt in the ashes. He raised his face to
the paling day. Are you there? he whispered. Will I
see you at last? Have you a neck by which to throttle
you? Have you a heart? Damn you eternally have
you a soul? Oh God, he whispered. Oh God. (10)*

Or:

*He woke coughing and walked out so as not to wake
the child. Following a stone wall in the dark,
wrapped in his blanket, kneeling in the ashes like a
penitent. (56)*

Later:

*He knelt there wheezing softly, his hands on his
knees. I am going to die, he said. Tell me how I am to
do that. (187)*

Another school of philosophy that has influenced
McCarthy throughout his 55-year career is
Absurdism, which is interested in the tension
between the human need to find value, meaning
and order in the world and our inability to do so.
Absurdist writers have long been drawn to post-
apocalyptic scenarios, seeing the wasteland as a
metaphor for human existence. The great Irish
playwright and novelist Samuel Beckett, for
example, set one of his famous absurdist plays,
Endgame, in what many critics have seen as a
post-nuclear wasteland; a world in which, as in the
world of *The Road,* there is "no more nature". *The
Road* has many similarities with the works of
Samuel Beckett. Compare, for example, these
sentences from a late Beckett story, "Lessness":
"Grey sky no cloud no sound no stir earth ash grey

sand... Ash grey all sides earth sky as one all sides endlessness" – with this sentence from *The Road*: "No moon rose beyond the murk and there was nowhere to go"(70). They could be part of the same work. *Endgame* dramatises, too, the tension between an inability to imagine a universe without God and an inability to believe in him: at one point a character called Hamm, after trying to pray and getting no response, shouts: "The bastard! He doesn't exist!"

According to the French absurdist philosopher, playwright and novelist Albert Camus, the individual has three options when addressing the meaninglessness of the universe: suicide, religious belief or acceptance. Because of his love for his son, suicide is not an option for the man, and he seems incapable of accepting meaninglessness. So he spends much of the novel groping after religious belief. This is why he has invented the concept of "carrying the fire". The fire doesn't "represent" anything in particular (it is not a symbol arrived at beforehand). It is a story that the man tells both his son and himself in order to give their life meaning – in order to give them a reason to carry on living in a "godless" world. What it represents is – almost – irrelevant. It is a stay against suicidal despair. It is the first spark of a new mythology in a new world. From mythology comes religion; from religion comes morality; from morality comes civilisation. The fire, in other words, represents nothing more nor less than the hope of a future.

The 19th-century Danish philosopher Soren Kierkegaard is often referred to as the father of Absurdism. But he was also a Christian and he emphasised the importance of a *personal* relationship with God, governed by individual choice rather than tradition or the church. I think McCarthy subscribes to Kierkegaard's philosophy. Recently, in his interview with Oprah Winfrey, when she asked if he'd "worked out the God thing, or not, yet", he replied: "Sometimes it's good to pray. I don't think you need to have a clear idea of who or what God is to pray." For Kierkegaard, God is not an otherworldly being, some alien presence riding above and distant from our world. For him, God is love – is love – and it is in the act of loving that we directly experience the divine. Perhaps, in *The Road*, the father's love for his son, in other words, is sacred. *Is* God.

Back to the question about the family at the end, then: are they his salvation or a false hope? There's no definitive answer. But the penultimate paragraph is significant:

The woman when she saw him put her arms around him and held him. Oh, she said, I am so glad to see you. She would talk to him sometimes about God. He tried to talk to God but the best thing was to talk to his father and he did talk to him and he didn't forget. The woman said that was all right. She said that the breath of God was his breath yet though it pass from man to man through all of time.

Here, the woman suggests that the boy's imaginative relationship with his deceased father is equivalent to a relationship with God. She sounds rather like Kierkegaard. Could it really be that *The Road* ends on a positive note about the transcendence of human love?

One last question: is the end of the novel an ending or a beginning? The past tense of the narrative voice and the penultimate paragraph quoted above certainly imply a future time from which to look back, though neither necessarily suggests a long or positive future. Are there other clues in the text?

There's a heartbreaking moment which touches on it. The man has carved his son a flute, on which to play, a "formless music for the age to come. Or perhaps the last music on earth called up from out of the ashes of its ruin"(81). When, some time later, he asks the boy where the flute is, the boy responds: "I threw it away"(169). The suggestion is that perhaps the father's notion of a music for *an age to come* – of, in fact, an age to come at all – is a misplaced sentimentalisation attached to the old world. The boy is not interested.

But then, elsewhere, his hope for the future seems warranted. When, early in the novel, he finds an unopened can of coke and gives it to the boy, the boy offers to share it. The man refuses it. "It's because I won't ever get to drink another one isn't it?" asks the boy. "Ever's a long time," the man replies (23). At this early stage in the novel, his words ring hollow; the hope seems false. Yet a hundred or so pages later they come across an underground stash of supplies: food, drink, bedding etc. Amongst the treasure they find is, lo and behold, a supply of coke – which they drink. Perhaps the man's hope, the suggestion is, was not misplaced.

Whatever conclusion you draw from the deliberately open-ended ending, something has been lost that can never be recovered. Here is McCarthy's extraordinary final paragraph:

Once there were brook trout in the streams in the mountains. You could see them standing in the amber current where the white edges of their fins wimpled softly in the flow. They smelled of moss in your hand. Polished and muscular and torsional. On their backs were vermiculate patterns that were maps of the world in its becoming. Maps and mazes. Of a thing which could not be put back. Not be made right again. In the deep glens where they lived all things were older than man and they hummed of mystery.

A SHORT CHRONOLOGY

1933 July 20 Born in Providence, Rhode Island

1965 Random House publishes *The Orchard Keeper*, McCarthy's first novel

1968 *Outer Dark*

1973 *Child of God*

1979 *Suttree*

1993 *All the Pretty Horses* wins National Book Award

2000 Film adaptation of *All the Pretty Horses*

2005 *No Country for Old Men*

2006 *The Road*

2007 McCarthy wins the Pulitzer Prize Film adaptation of *No Country for Old Men*

2009 Film adaptation of *The Road*

FURTHER READING

Arnold, Edwin T., and Dianne C. Luce, eds. *A Cormac McCarthy Companion: The Border Trilogy*. Jackson: UP of Mississippi, 2001.

Bell, Vereen M. *The Achievement of Cormac McCarthy*. Baton Rouge: Louisiana State UP,1988.

Chollier, Christine, ed. Cormac McCarthy: *Uncharted Territories/ Territoires Inconnus*. UP of Reims: Reims, France, 2003.

Cooper, Lydia R. *No More Heroes: Narrative Perspective and Morality in Cormac McCarthy*. Baton Rouge: Louisiana State UP, 2011.

Ellis, Jay. *No Place for Home: Spatial Constraint and Character Flight in the Novels of Cormac McCarthy*. New York: Routledge, 2006.

Greenwood, Willard P. *Reading Cormac McCarthy*. Santa Barbara, CA: Greenwood P, 2009.

Josyph, Peter. *Adventures in Reading Cormac McCarthy*. Lanham MD: Scarecrow P, 2010

Wallach, Rick, ed. *Myth, Legend, Dust: Critical Responses to Cormac McCarthy*. Manchester: Manchester UP, 2000.

Notes

Notes

First published in 2016 by
Connell Guides
Artist House
35 Little Russell Street
London WC1A 2HH

10 9 8 7 6 5 4 3 2 1

Picture credits:

p.13 © Everett/REX Shutterstock
p.31 © Everett/REX Shutterstock

A CIP catalogue record for this book is available from the British Library.
ISBN 978-1-907776-99-1

Design © Nathan Burton
Written by David Isaacs
Edited by Jolyon Connell

Assistant Editors and typeset by
Paul Woodward and Holly Bruce

www.connellguides.com